MY INVENTORY
THE BOOK

"It's time for a change; out with the old and in with the new.
Let go and let God!"

Earlene Michelle Robateau

My Inventory
Copyright © 2013 by Earlene Michelle Robateau
ISBN: 978-0615894478

Printed in the United States of America

"The Lord is my light and my salvation; whom shall I fear? The Lord is the strength of my life; whom shall I be afraid?"

Psalm 27:1

I dedicate this book to my husband, John. Thank you for always being there and supporting me.

My children, I thank God for each of you. Amanda, Amber, and Jonathan. I love you guys. Every day I thank the Lord for my blessing. Keep reaching high and never give up trust God and put God first.

My mother, Thelma Johnson thank you for everything I love you for the woman that you are and for always giving me a word to stand on.

To my father, the late Curtis Johnson, thank you.

My mother in-law Lois C. Robateau and to the late John O. Robateau thank you guys for the wonderful relationship that we have.

My sisters; Joyce, Donna, Patricia, Valerie, and the late Yvonne I thank you guys. I love each one of you from the bottom of my heart God has truly brought us a long way.

My brothers; Clifford, Ricky, Peter and the late Larry and Curtis Thank you, I love you guys.

My nephews and nieces I love you guys never stop going after your dreams and never stop believing God bless you all.

My friends and mentors; I love you all. May God bless each and every one of you.

Contents:

Introduction:
My Inventory

This book is for anyone that is looking to renew their Mind, Body, and Spirit.

Letting go of the pain as you look at your life you see, heartache sadness, fear, pain, jealousy, low self-esteem and so much more that has caused you to hold on to the baggage. You must learn how not to let your situation allow you to feel hopeless don't have a pity party for all of the things that happen in your life.

Let God have his way in your life.

Prayer
Lord, Thank you for guiding us and letting us know that we can't hold on to our past we must let go of it and give it to you lord I know you will give us peace in our life. In Jesus name Amen.

Let Go and Let God

Have you ever thought why you are at a certain place in your life when everything seems to be going wrong? Many people are in a place in their lives that they are stuck.

Sometimes life can be overwhelming, you may feel like waving the white flag to tell the world that you have given up with the demands of trying to be the perfect person that caused you to worry.

Chapter 1:
Monday
Dealing with Anxiety

Worry only brings on so many other problems to face in life. Sickness, Disease, Mental Illness, Strokes, Heart Attacks, etc. That will have you confined and afraid to move forward in life Jesus tells us not to worry about not having enough, clothing and food. We're going to go through something's in life but we must lean on our faith.

"Therefore I say unto you, take no thought for your life, what ye shall eat, or what ye shall put on. Is not the life more than meat, and the body than raiment?"

Matthew 6:25

"Take therefore no thought for the morrow; for the morrow shall take thought for the things of itself. Sufficient unto the day is the evil thereof."

Matthew 6:34

Prayer:
Lord, we thank you for teaching us not to worry, Lord you promise to supply all our needs. In Jesus name Amen.

"Remember ye not the former things,
neither consider the things of old."

Isaiah 43:18

God will be with you and see you through the
storm /rain /sunshine and the pain.

God is with you he knows just what you need he
will always be there for you. Lord, We thank you

Chapter 2
Tuesday
Dealing with Forgiveness

"Blessed is he whose transgression is forgiven. Whose sin is covered.
Blessed is the man unto whom the lord imputeth not iniquity, and in whose spirit there is no guile."

Psalm 32:1:2

We can have joy when we ask for forgiveness and to forgive the people that have done us wrong. When we show forgiveness it lets people see God working in us.

HOLD
ON

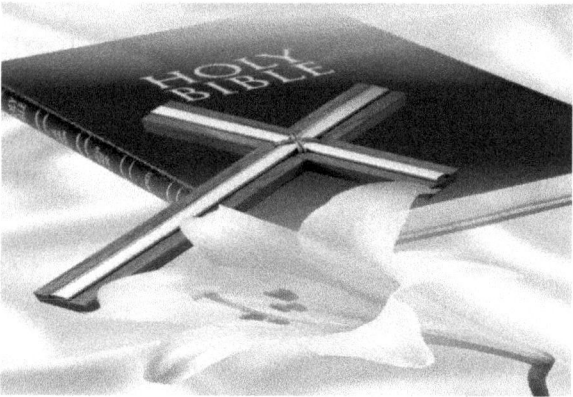

BELIEVE,
HAVE
FAITH

GOD
HAS
A
PLAN
FOR
YOU

Let Go and Let God!

NO more putting yourself down about your past. It stops today from your childhood until now let it go take back your life from the blame game, It's time to heal no more pointing the finger and allowing a person or thing to hold you back by saying "You did this, I couldn't help it, or I can't give it up. No one knows I've been living a lie or everyone is doing it or has done it or if you only knew my past."

Prayer:
Lord, NO more feeling sorry for ourselves we have the strength to let go because you are with us. Lord, our past doesn't keep us from moving forward in to the future. NO, more we give our past to you Lord' In Jesus Name. Amen.

Have you ever used these words before? I'm not good enough for that. Lying to yourself so you can feel good about your life even though deep down inside you're hurting facing trials and temptation; wondering how you can escape from it. Let Go, Let God and allow yourself to heal from the hurt, pain, and disappointment.

You can't lay down from years of hurt and pain never allow your problems or hardships to cause you to give up on yourself; live for now don't live in the past of the things that has caused you pain.

Prayer

Lord I must stop with the words that I allow to come out of my mouth. Please Lord help me I can't do it anymore Lord please teach me not to speak these words. In Jesus Name, Amen

"Have MERCY upon me, O God, according to thy lovingkindness: according unto the multitude of thy tender mercies blot out my transgressions.

2; Wash me thoroughly from mine iniquity, and cleanse me from my sin.

3; For I acknowledge my transgressions: and my sin is ever before me.

4; Against thee, thee only, have I sinned, and done this evil in thy sight: that thou mightest be justified when thou speakest, and be clear when thou judgest.

5; Behold, I was sharpen in iniquity; and in sin did my mother conceive me.

6 ; Behold , thou desirest truth in the inward parts: and in the hidden part thou shalt make me to know wisdom." Psalm 51; 1-6

God can change what seem Unchangeable

"To EVERY thing there is a season,
and a time to every purpose under The
heaven."

Ecclesiastes 3:1

Wasting Time

There are 365 days in a year, 24 hours in a day and seven days in the week. Have you ever wondered how much time we waste on Worrying, Complaining being Unhappy, Angry, Bitter, Selfish, Jealous, towards yourself or others?

When do we say enough is enough? going through life on a wheel like a hamster just running and wasting time focusing on all of the negative things in our life. Why do we do these things?

We have good days and bad days trying to deal with the circumstances in our life all on our own Wasting time looking for the Perfect Mate , Job, Body , Home, Family and Perfect Neighborhood. As women we have so many jobs in the home and outside the home taking care of the family.

What about the stay at home mom? We always forget about them and they just want to be heard and want respect. To the stay at home mom you must find time for yourself so you can be able to enjoy your family with a healthy mind, body, and spirit.

You can't take care of a family when you are burned out. Make a to do list keeping yourself healthy and fit don't lose yourself there's 365 days of the year make time for yourself it's a must and time to serve god and help others.

Men go out to work every day to provide for their family in the back of their minds they are wondering if it will ever be enough time to make more money for their family wanting to be the Perfect , Dad, Husband and leader for his family. Just know that God has it under control keep on providing for your family and never give up.

Some children try to be part of the "in crowd" just to get all the attention never mind if it's Negative or Positive just wanting to be perfect or getting in to trouble just to receive the approval from friends. Wasting time not knowing how to love themselves because no one ever showed them how to love or give them love.

Now they're adults with anger. Don't hold on to the past Love God and yourself.

Chapter 3
Wednesday
Dealing with Healing

"But he was wounded for our transgressions, he was bruised for our iniquities: the chastisement of our peace was upon him; and with his stripes we are healed. Isaiah 53:5

POEM
From Unbalanced to being Balance In life
From being Unhappy to happy
From being Unloved to loved
From being Uncontent to Content
Never be afraid to look in the mirror
And learn to love the person that you see
looking back at you. Love what you
see which is Gods beauty and that is you.

Never be afraid to say I am sorry or to let go to the person that has hurt you. Never believe that God has left you when you are going through your struggles allow it to be an opportunity for strength and growth in your faith.

Trust God he'll supply all your needs it is easy to blame others for what has happened in your life and some of it may be true but why give a person some much time in your life by holding on to the pain. Time waits for no one let it go. "For to be carnally minded is death; but to be spiritually minded is life and peace."

Romans 8; 6

"Delight yourself in the Lord; and he will give you the desires of your heart."

Psalms 37; 4

Seasons come and go all year long and we are all cleaning and preparing for the next season. Putting things away taking things out of storage and there's nothing wrong with that but if you were to do an inventory of your life and start cleaning it up you would be surprised at all the clutter. That you have mentally and physically
In your life. There's a season to laugh, there is a season to cry, a season to fast, a season to let go ,a season to grow a season to die, a season to be born, a season to be still, a season to listen, a season to serve ,a season to work. Everything has a season and everyone has their season it's what you do

when you are in your season. Let God help you though your season.

Remember These Three Words
POEM
STOP / / LOOK //LISTEN

STOP: To take a moment to see what's in front of you don't allow yourself to be so focused on your past that you can't see what's around you.

LOOK: We must learn to look at what we have and be grateful take a deep breath and look at Gods beautiful creation and take it all in from the sky to the grass on the ground the colors in the flowers and trees Smile when you look at all of Gods beauty Smile because God is smiling at you.

LISTEN: Take time out to pray and ask for forgiveness ask for wisdom and understanding learn to listen when someone is speaking to us we don't have to be the ones talking all the time. Sometimes you should be still and listen to what God is saying to you through prayer.

"for the LORD seeth not as man seeth; for man looketh on the outward appearance, but the LORD looketh on the heart".

1 Samuel 16:7

Chapter 4
Thursday
Dealing with Hurt

"Behold, God is mine helper: the Lord is
with them that uphold my soul."

Psalms 54; 4

Doing an inventory of your life is to help you
see there's no one perfect and everyone makes
mistakes stop being hard on yourself. Wondering
if you are good enough holding on to the pain
feeling let down like no one cares for you. You
must deal with the pain that have caused you to
hurt maybe you have been raised in a bad
neighborhood or was bullied when you were a
child or dealing with mental and physical abuse
God knows your pain and who you are and what
you have been through. We must learn to trust
God and make a change with God you can do it.

Don't allow people to tell you that you can't make
it in life. Because of your past, maybe you had a
drug addiction or was an alcoholic or never
finished school and always wanted to go back or
want to start a new career, or business. God has
given you a purpose in life and it's not about
worrying about your past. It's about serving don't

wait for someone to help you. You must start by helping others, learn to give back use your past issues as a learning opportunity to help someone get through a time in their life.

6; Be careful for nothing but in everything by
prayer and supplication with thanks giving
let your request's be made known unto God.
7; And the peace of God which passeth all
understanding shall keep your hearts and minds
through Christ Jesus.
Philippian 4:6-7

Chapter 5
Friday
Dealing with Prayer

First start by praying, asking God for forgiveness and allow the lord to speak to you through this journey. Learn how to let go, remember don't hold on to the past you can't go back and fix everything that has happened in your life ten or maybe twenty years ago you must learn how to move on and give it to God he knows what is best for you.

THE LORD'S PRAYER

"After this manner there-fore pray ye;

Our Father which art in heaven, Hallowed be thy name.
Thy Kingdom come. Thy will be done in earth, it is in heaven.
Give us this day our daily bread.
And forgive us our debts, as we forgive our debtors,
And lead us not into temptation, but deliver us from
evil; For thine is the kingdom, and the power, and the glory, forever. Amen."

Matthew 6:9 - 13

Confess your faults one to another, that ye may be healed. The effectual fervent prayer of a righteous man availeth much. James 5:16

I had some challenges along the way in my life. I never met my father, my mother was pregnant with me when my father died of a heart attack.

As a little girl to now a grown woman married with children. I had always wondered why I was the one that never met my father I was hurting inside with the emotional pain that I was feeling. I could no longer keep that pain inside and all the other things that people have done to me.

I had to learn I must give it to God and to go looking for it in people and things that was not the answer. I was very tired and afraid of not belonging or fitting in but now. I know I had to change and the change came from God on the inside and he can change you.

Don't worry if you can't go back to change some things in your life. Things would be better perhaps but don't waste time on what if or I should have done or maybe. Sometimes you can be holding yourself back from your dreams and goals. You may think that this is weird or funny or just strange.

I started to take a real good look at my life to see how can I change the way I'm feeling towards myself and others to be a better person. Let's look at life as an onion you just have to peel back the layers to uncover who you really are, you're going to cry and you may even laugh.

When you're finished you will discover that you are a child of God and he has made you in his image.

HAPPINESS

"Rejoice in the Lord al-ways; and
again I say, Rejoice."

Philippians 4:4

Chapter 6
Saturday
SCRIPTURES THAT ARE HELPFUL

"So God created man in his own image, in the image of God created he him; male and
Female created he them."

Genesis 1:27

So stop being hard on yourself about who you are and what you look like and not having enough.

It's is impossible for man to be perfect that's why it's important for you to have a relationship with God. He loves you just the way you are.

"For ye are all the children of God by faith in Christ Jesus."

Galatians 3:26

Cry your last cry let go let God Laugh when no one else is Laughing, Dance like no one is watching. When you fall get back up love God love yourself love everyone even those that hurt you.

"For with God nothing shall be impossible"

Luke 1: 37

We see God is able and he'll give you strength don't walk by sight walk by Faith.

"Now faith is the substance of things hoped for evidence of thing's not seen."

Hebrews 11:1

I know God does not want us to be lost or unhappy in life he wants us to be happy and making a joyful noise unto to him.

PRAYER

Lord, thank you for everything show us Lord to look to you for the happiness and joy.

"Make a joyful noise unto the lord all ye lands.
2; Serve the lord with gladness; come before his presence with singing.
3; Know ye that the lord he is God, It is he that hath made us, and not we ourselves; we are his people, and the sheep of his pasture.
4; Enter into his gates with thanksgiving and into his courts with praise; be thankful unto him, and bless his name.
5; for the lord is good; his mercy is everlasting and his truth endureth to all generations."

Psalm 100;

Chapter 7
Sunday Dealing With Love

"But the fruit of the Spirit is
love, joy, peace, longsuffering,
gentleness, goodness, faith,"

Galatians 5:22

My Inventory My Story

The change came when I decide to the inventory
of my life I started removing things and people
that caused harm and didn't mean any good in my
life. I prayed and asked God for direction and to
put me under construction to allow me to be
restore from inside-out. The love that he has given
me. I thank him every day and I share his love with
everyone. I am more kind, caring with what he has
given me I look at everything in my life so
different now you must get to know him with his
love you can have Peace, Joy, Happiness, Wisdom
and Understanding.

"And be not conformed to this world; but be ye
transformed by the renewing of your mind,
that ye may prove what is that good, and accept-
able, and perfect, will of God."

Romans 12:2

I always had a relationship with God but it was only when I needed something that's when I would only call on him in prayer and read the bible. When I had made my decision to let go and let God I knew God was calling me into the ministry but I still was holding on to my past but as I started to do my inventory of my life I was ready to let go of all of stuff that was causing me to be sick and be the person that God has called for me to be .I had it all wrong before now I put God first in my life and I am so grateful to God for his grace and mercy.

My life has changed I don't have to wonder who I am I know who I am. I am a child of God. I have changed and I know I have changed but this change didn't come from man it came from God. I am now a Wife, Mother, Minister, Hairstylist, Author and I believe with God he still has more in store for me.

Do your inventory of your life. Who are you ask yourself these question? What's holding me back? Or who's holding me back? never be afraid to tell your story and be content in your life God will give you what your heart desires.

God wants an attitude of service not an attitude of self service.

Remember where your strength is going to come from have faith and believe be confident and grateful that now you're ready to let go.
Don't give up hang in there.

> "He gives power to the tired and worn out and strength to the weak."
>
> Isaiah 40:29

TO BE IN HIS PRESENCE

> "Consider what I say; and Lord give thee understanding in all things."
>
> 2 Timothy 2:7

Thinking with God sometimes we must be in his presence so we can hear what God is telling us. When you find yourself so busy that you don't know when was the last time you gave him glory for just keeping you even when you didn't keep yourself From harm and danger even when you didn't know how you were going to make Ends meet, he still was working it out for you never be too busy to stop and take a moment to say thank you Lord;

Peace/ Understanding / Wisdom / Love and Joy and there's so much more happiness in your life and God has a better place for you don't walk around bitter let go and start your inventory.

God's love is beautiful embrace it you will never find love like God's trust me find time to be in his presence. POEM

I am BEAUTIFUL because of you.
I am LOVE because of you.
I am CARING because of you.
I am KIND because of you.
I am HAPPY because of you.
I am GIVING because of you.
I am THANKFUL because of you.
I am FORGIVING because of you.
I am at PEACE because of you. I
am WHO I am because of you.

I AM ALL THESE THINGS BECAUSE OF
YOU
LORD YOU MADE ME JUST LIKE YOU.

I love meditation it's a beautiful thing just a few minutes a day just you and the lord.

Find a quiet place and sit, close your eyes and be still breathe slow relax and take in the moment. Relax, Release, Relate.

Let go you will never know how good God is until you form a relationship with him study his word.

Prayer is the key that unlocks the door to faith it's time to clean up your life. Being in God's presence give it all to him Anger, Jealousy, Hate, and Self-doubt, past issues.

There's no problem too big for God put God first in everything that you do. I said it before and I'll say it again trust God take it one day at a time.

"Trust in the lord with all thine heart and lean not unto thine own understanding in all thy ways Acknowledge him, and he shall direct thy path."
                                                    Proverbs 3:5-6

PRAYER

Lord Thank you for everything now lord be with us on this journey as we go forward in life. Doing an Inventory of our lives So That We Can Be Ready in our Calling. In Jesus name Amen.

God Bless you
Meditate on his word

YOUR
JOURNEY
HAS
JUST
BEGUN

A POINT TO PONDER

I believe God has given everyone a gift and everyone's gift is different so be yourself think about your talent what dreams you have what is it that you want to do. Some may ask how can I clean up my life with the past I had who will give me a chance or I'm too old to follow my dreams and I don't know how to start ? These are the questions you don't allow to come in your mind. FEAR is not an Option.

Trust God

MY INVENTORY
JOURNAL

January

"I will bless the LORD at all times: his praise
shall continually be in my mouth."

Psalms 34:1

_____

_____

_____

_____

_____

_____

_____

_____

_____

_____

_____

_____

_____

_____

_____

_____

_____

_____

_____

_____

_____

_____

"I will bless the Lord at all time: his praise shall
continually be in my mouth." Psalms 34:1

_____
_____
_____
_____
_____
_____
_____
_____
_____
_____
_____
_____
_____
_____
_____
_____
_____
_____
_____
_____
_____
_____
_____
_____
_____

February

"I will not be afraid of ten thousands of people that have set themselves against me round about."

Psalms 3:6

_____
_____
_____
_____
_____
_____
_____
_____
_____
_____
_____
_____
_____
_____
_____
_____
_____
_____
_____
_____
_____
_____
_____
_____
_____

"I will not be afraid of ten thousands of people that have set themselves against me round about."
Psalms 3:6

March

"Confess your faults one to another, and pray one for another, that ye may be healed. The effectual fervent prayer of a righteous man availeth much."

James 5:16

"Confess your faults one to another, and pray one for another, that ye may be healed. The effectual fervent prayer of a righteous man availeth much."

James 5:16

_____
_____
_____
_____
_____
_____
_____
_____
_____
_____
_____
_____
_____
_____
_____
_____
_____
_____
_____

April

"My flesh and my heart may fail, but God is the strength of my heart and my portion forever."

Psalm 73:26

"My flesh and my heart may fail, but God is the strength of my heart and my portion forever."

Psalm 73:26

_____
_____
_____
_____
_____
_____
_____
_____
_____
_____
_____
_____
_____
_____
_____
_____
_____
_____
_____
_____
_____
_____
_____
_____

May

"Fear thou not, for I am with thee: be not dismayed; for I am thy God: I will strengthen thee; yea, I will help thee; yea, I will uphold thee with the right hand of my righteousness."

Isaiah 41:10

"Fear thou not, for I am with thee: be not dismayed; for I am thy God: I will strengthen thee; yea, I will help thee; yea, I will uphold thee with the right hand of my righteousness."

Isaiah 41:10

_____
_____
_____
_____
_____
_____
_____
_____
_____
_____
_____
_____
_____
_____
_____
_____
_____
_____
_____
_____
_____
_____

June

"I can do all things through Christ which strengtheneth me."

Philippians 4:13

"I can do all things through Christ which strengtheneth me."

Philippians 4:13

_____
_____
_____
_____
_____
_____
_____
_____
_____
_____
_____
_____
_____
_____
_____
_____
_____
_____
_____
_____

_____
_____
_____

July

"And we know that all things work together for the good to them that love God, to them who are the called according to his purpose."

Roman 8:28

_____

_____

_____

_____

_____

_____

_____

_____

_____

_____

_____

_____

_____

_____

_____

_____

_____

_____

_____

_____

"And we know that all things work together for the good to them that love God, to them who are the called according to his purpose."

Roman 8:28

_____
_____
_____
_____
_____
_____
_____
_____
_____
_____
_____
_____
_____
_____
_____
_____
_____
_____
_____
_____
_____
_____
_____
_____
_____

August

"Make a joyful noise unto the LORD, all ye lands."

Psalm 100:1

"Make a joyful noise unto the LORD, all ye lands."

Psalm 100:1

September

"No weapon that is formed against thee shall prosper; and every tongue that shall rise against thee in judgment thou shalt condemn. This is the heritage of the servants of the LORD, and their righteousness is of me, saith the LORD.

Isaiah 54:17

_____
_____
_____
_____
_____
_____
_____
_____
_____
_____
_____
_____
_____
_____
_____
_____
_____

"No weapon that is formed against thee shall prosper; and every tongue that shall rise against thee in judgment thou shalt condemn. This is the heritage of the servants of the LORD, and their righteousness is of me, saith the LORD.

Isaiah 54:17

_

October

"Wait on the LORD: be of good courage, and he shall strengthen thine heart: wait, I say, on the LORD."

Psalm 27:14

_____

_____

_____

_____

_____

_____

_____

_____

_____

_____

_____

_____

_____

_____

_____

_____

_____

_____

"Wait on the LORD: be of good courage, and he shall strengthen thine heart: wait, I say, on the LORD."

Psalm 27:14

_____
_____
_____
_____
_____
_____
_____
_____
_____
_____
_____
_____
_____
_____
_____
_____
_____
_____
_____
_____
_____

November

"He that dwelleth in the secret place of the most High shall abide under the shadow of the Almighty.

I will say of the Lord, He is my refuge and my fortress: my God in him will I trust."

Psalms 91:1-2

_____

_____

_____

_____

_____

_____

_____

_____

_____

_____

_____

_____

_____

_____

_____

_____

_____

_____

_____

_____

"He that dwelleth in the secret place of the most High shall abide under the shadow of the Almighty.

I will say of the Lord, He is my refuge and my fortress: my God in him will I trust."

Psalms 91:1-2

_____
_____
_____
_____
_____
_____
_____
_____
_____
_____
_____
_____
_____
_____
_____
_____
_____
_____
_____
_____

December

"I waited patiently for the LORD; and he inclined unto me, and heard my cry.

He brought me up also out of a horrible pit, out of the miry clay and set my feet upon a rock, and established my goings."

Psalms 40:1-2

_____

_____

_____

_____

_____

_____

_____

_____

_____

_____

_____

_____

_____

_____

_____

_____

_____

_____

"I waited patiently for the LORD; and he inclined unto me, and heard my cry.

He brought me up also out of a horrible pit, out of the miry clay and set my feet upon a rock, and established my goings."

Psalms 40:1-2

_____
_____
_____
_____
_____
_____
_____
_____
_____
_____
_____
_____
_____
_____
_____
_____
_____
_____
_____